A NOTE TO PARENTS ABOUT SNOOPING

Privacy is an important issue to most people. Snooping is one of the most offensive assaults on one's privacy as it is usually done in secret and therefore can not be addressed. Victims of snooping often feel violated and usually have difficulty maintaining positive regard for the perpetrator.

The purpose of this book is to teach children the importance of respecting another person's privacy. It is also to define snooping and to encourage children to avoid doing it.

By reading and discussing this book with your child, you can help him or her become trustworthy. This will go a long way toward helping your child formulate relationships that are built on mutual respect and trust.

Unless your reason for snooping is a matter of life or death, you should not snoop into your child's life or belongings. Instead, you should respect his or her privacy. By doing so, you will model an appropriate stance regarding snooping. When one is not invited to explore another person's thoughts, feelings, relationships, or belongings, he or she should not do so.

This book belongs to:

_____

Published by Scholastic Inc.
90 Old Sherman Turnpike, Danbury, CT 06816.

SCHOLASTIC and associated logos are trademarks and/or
registered trademarks of Scholastic Inc.

ISBN 0-7172-8581-2

First Scholastic Printing, October 2005

A Book About
Snooping

by
Joy Berry

SCHOLASTIC INC.

New York   Toronto   London   Auckland   Sydney
Mexico City   New Delhi   Hong Kong   Buenos Aires

This book is about Sam and his sister Maggie.

Reading about Sam and Maggie can help you understand and deal with **snooping.**

You are snooping when you secretly look through other people's things.

You are snooping when you secretly try to find out things about other people.

Snooping is being nosy in a sneaky, meddlesome way.

No one likes it when someone snoops.

It is important to treat others the way you want to be treated.

If you do not want others to snoop, you must not snoop.

It is important to *respect other people*. Do not secretly listen in when others are talking together.

Do not secretly listen in when someone is talking on the telephone.

Do not watch other people without their knowing it.

Do not pry into another person's business. Do not try to learn things about others that they might not want you to know.

It is important to *respect other people's property.* Do not look in the windows or doors of people's houses without their knowing it.

Do not go into other people's homes unless you have permission. Do not go into a room in another person's home unless you have permission.

If a door is closed, knock on it and wait to be invited before you go in.

Do not look through another person's dresser drawers, cupboards, or closets unless you have permission.

Do not read things that belong to another person unless you have permission.

It is important *to respect other people's privacy.* People might have some thoughts and feelings they want to keep to themselves.

Do not try to make people share the thoughts and feelings they do not want to share.

If you snoop, others might feel they cannot depend on you. They might feel they cannot trust you.

Snooping can be harmful to you and others. It is not good for you or for the people around you.

It is important to treat other people the way you want to be treated.

If you do not want other people to snoop, you must not snoop.